Pictures That Got Small

Pictures That Got Small

Poems by James Brock

WordTech Editions

Published by WordTech Editions
P.O. Box 541106
Cincinnati, OH 45254-1106

Typeset in Baskerville by WordTech Communications LLC,
Cincinnati, OH

ISBN: 1932339841
LCCN: 2004114222

Poetry Editor: Kevin Walzer
Business Editor: Lori Jareo

Visit us on the web at www.wordtechweb.com

Cover Photo: "Drive-In," courtesy of The Florida
Photographic Collection of the Florida State Archives.

Acknowledgments

To the academy, I would like to thank the editors of the following publications in which some of the poems appeared in early formations:

88
Caffeine Destiny
Gulf Stream
MiPoesis
North American Review
Snakebird: Thirty Years of Anhinga Poets
storySouth
Tigertail
ZC Portal

Thank you for your friendship and inspiration, Joe Pacheco, Marilyn Koren, Barb Finkelstein, Rick Campbell, Sylvia Curbelo, Lola Haskins, Mia Leonin, Jill Drumm, and Michael Hettich—everyone of you the always beautiful and wild ingenue in my Florida featurette. And to all those wonderful people out there in the dark, I am most grateful.

as ever, for Gerri and Carson,
the stars of my matinee,

and with gratitude for Jesse and Lyn,
for their cameo appearances in my life,
and the wise people who love them foolishly

I am big. It's the pictures that got small.

Norma Desmond (Gloria Swanson), *Sunset Boulevard*

Contents

I. How the Trouble Starts

I can tell you something about this place. The boys around here call
it "The Black Lagoon." Only they say nobody has ever come back
alive to prove it.

Lucas (Nestor Pavia), *The Creature from the Black Lagoon*

Killing the Exotics

First, my backyard, the Cuban laurel
tree, neither Cuban nor laurel, would be
a good start, but with its
leaf and creeper, it keeps the St. Augustine
grass at bay. So I am left to contemplate
the killing of the other exotics, the available
snake plants, those variegated swords with
tendrilled tubers, and thus I have begun to go
native in Florida. Sure, I have
thinned the ligustrums and shell-ginger lily,
sheared the croton, but I am still learning
the names of exotics: you, carrotwood, you corn
plant, you bird of paradise and
jacaranda, you bougainvillea, frangipani,
banana, Hong Kong orchid tree, you
umbrella plant and Mexican heather, you Surinam
cherry and valencia orange, and you
weeping bottlebrush and you whatever,
all of you an Ohioed dream of Florida, so much backdrop
for *The Creature from the Black Lagoon*, I say
must go. But who would
not want that kind of 3-D Florida
in 1954, to be startled
by it, after a hard day of filming, even if it's just
a B-movie, to be Ben Chapman, spending six
hours latexed in a modified diving suit, half
an alligator boy's body from the roadside
attraction and the rest a Chinatown fish-dragon's
head, carrying around slinky Julia Adams all day,
and finally unzipping the gill-man's mask,
freeing his head to the subtropic air
and light? Of course, what Ben Chapman
wants first is a good smoke, then a high-ball,
and the next day a round of golf, a trip
to Palm Beach for a quick fuck, and he
thinks he could very well live here, forget
Pasadena and snap up that tiny

bungalow in Sanibel, grow mangoes and oranges
and Brazilian pepper, and go fishing
out in the Gulf of Mexico.
What might he leave after he goes? A Florida worth a little
killing? Today, I believe my neighbor's bishofia
might be an even better start,
save for that downy woodpecker, behind me, holed up
in the dead arm of the Cuban laurel tree,
that
one-ounced brute, eyeing me.

My Black Lagoon

I lack the imagination,
         so my lagoon is nothing more
than Wakulla Springs, 1954, black

and white, tropical in a Johnny
         Weissmueller kind of way, with rubber
creepers strung among the live

oak and cabbage palms, and
         recordings of screeching macaws
and gibbon monkeys dubbed in

later by the studio's foley crew. But
         my Black Lagoon is not the love-nest
of one gill-man. For in Florida,

reptilian life is fecund, especially
         for the exotic, and so what is good
for the caiman, the walking catfish,

and the hydrangea, is good
         for the gill-creatures. In their lair
tread scores of gill-men and gill-

women, leaving traces and tracks
         for young, nubile, and pre-sexual
scientists, white men and women

in bathing suits, who follow them
         and get caught. Once captured,
the human swoons and faints

and wakens, compelled to touch
         this gill skin, not at all slimy
or rough, but supple and living

gill-woman and gill-man flesh
    that shivers against human breath,
that warms against the brush

   of a woman's firming nipple
    or a man's soft lower lip,
so that the gill cock hardens

   and the gill cunt darkens
    and moistens. They look
upon the human, comb back

   the tassel of wet hair from
    the human's face, to suggest that
the gill-woman is ready, the gill-man

   is ready. At that moment,
    the human decides then
never to leave the lair,

   but to ignore the old colleagues
    who cry out some mono-syllabic
name, as this human's mouth

   itself opens, not for a sound,
    but for a new kind of breathing,
a different kind of depth.

Her Silvermoon Café

Sleep and you have astronomy,
or maybe her Silvermoon Café,

where you cannot find your brother,
the twelve-step pornographer,
or your brother,
the de-barred embezzler,
or your brother,
the post-Victorian oboist.

Sleep and you have astronomy,
or maybe her Silvermoon Café,

where you cannot find your sister,
the shop-lifting enabler,
or your sister,
the special educationist stripper,
or your sister,
the merchant marine chemist.

Sleep and you have astronomy,
or maybe her Silvermoon Café,

where someone else has snapshot
three women laughing, beneath
the shack's sign, a crescent moon
and star—is this a still from
a Hollywood set? Or you could believe
the women are swamp mermaids,
and there's no need saying
voluptuous mermaids at that.
Of course, with mermaids
in any poem, you have to think
of T.S. Eliot's mermaids not singing
to him, but who would be surprised
at that? And would you not hear
the laughter, too, rising to the ceiling

of your sleep, firing nebulae, star
matter, and gravity? Whose laughter,
then? And what is that you do
when you sleep and wrong the world?

Upon Hearing That My Grant Application Was Passed Over and the Winner Was a Bio-Tech Professor Who Has Designed Genetically-Altered Protein for Buckwheat Seed

—for Denise

Okay, call me Tallulah Bankhead. I wanted that award,
the crystal glass eagle, the pendant, the certificate,
the lapel pin, the thousand bucks, and the parking space
next to the university president's spot—the whole
platinum and sapphire tiara. I knew I should have
written that poem on the manipulations
of amino acid balance in buckwheat seed proteins.
I knew I should have named that new genetic
strand *Omicron-Brockide-32*, should have brokered
the patent rights to Monsanto, let them spread the seed
of my pumped-up, high-octane, drought-tolerant,
American-can-do-know-how buckwheat
to sub-Sahara Africa and southern Mongolia.

One year later, then, I would have written
the grant report, presented it to the committee
on PowerPoint, and finished off my presentation
with a streaming video clip, showing some adolescent
boy, from Gambia, say, and he would be eating
my buckwheat flat bread, and there he would be,
digitalized, smiling, full, and muscular. Yes,
and at that moment, vindicated and wise,
teary-eyed and generous, the grant committee
would gather and lift me on their shoulders, laughing
and singing, joyful for all the corporate sponsorships that
would follow me and bless our humble home
institution. For me, dare I dream further confirmations?
O, to be Nationally Endowed, Guggenheimed, MacArthured!

Of course, in Gambia, and other geographies
beneath the sweep and hoozah of fellowships
and announcements in *The Chronicle of Higher Education*,
the newly nourished could be striking the flint
of their first syllables of their first poems, poems
whose phrases—under the most subdued of flames—would
coolly scorch and burn our best American intention.

Sun Valley Serenade (1941)

For the black ice number, the choreographer
writes his dance on Sonja Henie, marks
        where she will commit to one final spin,
picking her toe to stop, smiling directly

to the camera. The trick: how to keep
the movement slow, so as not to slice
        into the black ice, dyed with ink, spitting
onto her outfit, which must be white,

and her hair, which must be blonde.
And for this year, 1940, late fall, Idaho
        is Hollywood, two years after Averell Harriman
has opened the resort—and also in

production, it's *A Woman's Face*, and
Joan Crawford walks through an exterior
        shot. Through this early winter snow
she leaves the doctor's office, her scar

erased by surgery: the woman with the
cold heart becomes the beautiful woman
        with the cold heart, a monster, declares
Melvyn Douglas, the surgeon in love with

his work. It's Gary Cooper visiting Hemingway
for goose hunting, and they will return later
        in the season, when the Nicholas Brothers
and Glenn Miller and Dorothy Dandridge

have arrived, although Hemingway will say
how the only Negress artist remains Josephine
        Baker, and Coop will tell Hemingway
there he goes again, all full of Paris. Hemingway

will get the last word, that Paris and war
gave Gary Cooper his greatest role.
                    For the movie stars, nothing but to stroll
        the Sun Valley Inn, loiter by the outdoor

        ice rink at night, as the director of photography
reads his light meter against the black ice,
                    what Zanuck had ordered specifically for this movie.
        Henie's a tired franchise already, but still on

        contract. "Make the ice look like a floor,
something that Rogers and Astaire would glide
                    over." But he budgets $7000 for the scene, enough
        for two days of shooting, and nothing more.

        For the final take, it's Henie in her last available
outfit, the other costumes stained
                    from the falls, the ink beading in its freezing,
        and she cries to her director, it's "grooty,"

        meaning "gritty" or "grouty," but he has
seen this panic before, and Zanuck has warned him,
                    too, of Henie in particular, all
        excuses and ermine, and so it's Henie,

        and she's on her final spin, crisp
through and through, the spin tightening,
                    and before she cleats the ice, everyone
        can see the centrifuged run of ink

        lip her skirt, see the two days
in the tank, and she sees it, too, still
                    in her spinning, but why not keep the spinning,
        with all these lights, all these people?

        And she owes them everything, waiting
through war and Depression and boredom.
                    She owes them some Olympian razz-a-ma-tazz,
        something that will make someone in

the audience gasp *oh*. What's a goddess for?
Who cares if it's Zanuck's show? His lousy dime?
Why not deliver the real goods this time?
Hit it, Sonja! Hit it!

How the Trouble Starts

Laurel and Hardy carry an upright piano
        through the streets of New York, American
                mongrels nipping at them, avoiding street
        vendors and cops, passing between
horse carts and trolley cars and model A's,

across the Brooklyn bridge, down to the harbor
        and its fish markets and teamsters, finding their way
                up a ramp and onto a freighter,
        across the Atlantic, making their
way through the lower decks and

cargo holdings, through cattle and farm
        machinery, until they reach the upper
                deck, rollicking with the waves, as a sailor
        pecks "Daisy" on the piano, while
Laurel and Hardy keep their grip of it, as the

freighter passes through the Straits
        of Gibraltar, and deep into the Mediterranean,
                and then marching off the ship onto some sunny
        Italian port, winnowing between fat men and women
selling bread and pasta, children playing soccer,

with Florentine dogs nipping at them,
        through the southern Alps and onto
                the roads of a snowy Tyrolean village, amid
        goats and men in lederhosen dallying
about, a small oom-pah band, all brass and

drum, shadowing them, as a pretty Swiss Miss,
        all blonde and busom, plays a little
                Für Elise on the piano, and then
        quickly up the Matterhorn, thousands of feet
above some Alpine field, dotted with

chalets and sheep, to a wooden bridge,
      suspended all the way to Mount Blanc, with
         missing and broken planks, frayed
    ropes, but they don't miss a step.
Mid-way on the bridge is a gorilla.

II. Matthew Barney Suite

O consolations of the craft.
How we put
the old poultices to the old sores,
the same mirrors to the old magic.

Eavan Boland, "Listen. This Is the Noise of Myth"

Bronco Stadium 3

A denuded Boise night backdrop,
Lyle Smith Field lighted, rounded
by the empty aluminum and concrete

Bronco Stadium, where else? 80 chorus girls
glide over the blue astro-turf,
orange and white belled, white legged,

perennially radial smiles. It's Ziegfield
without the feathers, but still icy, crisp,
scrubbed women. Above,

two Goodyear Blimps, gray and star-flecked,
and through the round portals, the faces
of four attendants, or maybe pilots,

blowing cigarette smoke through
their nostrils, watching the chorus line,
one thin white line, quickly pulse and

flash beneath them. The attendants have no
one to attend, or the pilots have no flight
plan issued. And if they did,

they'd still be circling the 'o' of Bronco Stadium,
circling the 'o' of Boise,
the 'o' of Idaho. And on the white

centerpiece, one mound of green grapes in
Goodyear Blimp O, and one mound of
red grapes in Goodyear Blimp OO.

Beneath the table's funneled leg, Miss Goodyear,
our heroine, slinks, all lingerie
and plastic pumps and silk, a Gil Elvgren

sylvan pin-up. She pulls from her blonde
hair a bobby pin, works the bobby pin
to drill a hole through which she

steals one grape at a time. The attendants
don't care. It is not their grapes.
Miss Goodyear pushes the grapes, one

by one, into whatever available orafice:
her mouth, her nostil, her anus, her vagina.
However entered, the grapes travel

the body Goodyear, warmed by the spleen's
blood, the ball gladder's bile, the fat
tissue's slow burning, through every duct

digestive, reproductive, respiratory,
until they find a channel through
the heel of her pump. They remain grapes

through and through. Miss Goodyear
collects them, lines them into shapes:
a hint of the areola, or maybe the ovaries,

the Fallopian tubes, or the uterus. Beneath
them, the attendants watch the chorus line
fan out, and when Miss Goodyear's grapes

suggest a shape, the chorus
girls follow: now they are the vulva, but not
quite, now the mesovarium, but not quite,

now the primary oocyte, but not quite,
now the ampulla, but not quite,
assimilating, dissolving, reassembling.

Do they tire? Do their kicks lose snap?
And above them, the Blimps remain
motionless, despite their loud

engines' droning, but the chorus girls
do not miss a step, or fade their
smiles in the least, and the

Blimps remain motionless, between
the opposing erect goalposts, where there
is no landing and no final coupling.

If Matthew Barney Were 6'3"

and not just a hair beneath 6 feet even,
too small for a Pac-10 recruiting coach
to take note and no decent college

in the Big Sky Conference, but let's say
Matthew Barney were three inches
taller, coming out, a Capital High Eagle,

a QB with a good arm and 1480 SAT, a quick
release, a quicker read, but not especially fast
on the field, or slippery, yet Berkeley would

have been interested, maybe UW, too, but
yes, UCLA or USC would have been a little
too much to wish for, and so in February,

Matthew signs his letter of intent for Cal.
Is this too much dreaming? A Boise kid
leading a Pac-10 team? Take Jake Plummer,

also a Capital High Eagle, just a few years
down, before he adopted Kenny Stabler's nickname,
at Arizona State—isn't that proof enough?

And if we take Jake *the Snake* Plummer, why not
a pro career for Matthew Barney? Why not a
mid-round draft pick? Let it even be

the Los Angeles Raiders, Al Davis
mining on the cheap and mean, so that
Matthew Barney arrives for summer training,

already signed, only a little starry over
Daryle Lamonica's pep talk to the rookies.
And he's good enough for the team,

beats out Vince Evans on the depth
charts, gets Vince's number 11, and 3 years
down, a starter for a season, and then traded

to Kansas City, and then a stint at Miami
with Jimmy Johnson, a little insurance
for Dan Marino. It'd be over fast enough,

an average, unspectacular journeyman's stay.
But while in Los Angeles, say in 1992,
when he starts, tosses a decent passing

rating of 87.8—okay, so it's Tim Brown's
work that inflates the stat—but
good enough that Hollywood notices,

especially after Matthew dons all black
shoes, shoestrings, stockings, masking
the silver stripes, and once, on a bootleg,

he skirts into the end zone, a five-yard run,
untouched, and he drops the ball,
lies down on the turf, arms down his side,

parallel to his number, kicks off his shoes,
brings his legs together and butterfly
kicks, a sperm in the L.A. Coliseum.

The Je-zoid Jocks won't get it,
all carried with their This-Glory's-
Yours-God Touchdowns, as they point

to the lights, drop to one knee, in this house
of the Lord. Art Shell must leave the sideline,
stands over Matthew, "Son, what's with you?"

And Matthew, Jesus, he's just a sperm,
ball-less head of genetic coding, flopping
on the o-less field, no ovum, no openings,

just a pre-man. But it gets noticed,
so that in April, he's at the Academy
Awards, escorting Miranda Richardson,

and there's talk of Jonathan Demme
talking of Matthew, but it's too much,
really. Besides, Matthew's already on his way

to Kansas City, where he learns
Marty Schottenheimer's game, where
Marcus Allen finds redemption, also exiled

from the Raiders, and Joe Montana,
too, where they become young men
again, boys, upon a prairie and near

a river where everything dissolves, devolves.
Marty takes Matthew under wing, sees that
there's a coach in Matthew's soul,

and even tells Matthew that, even
thumping Matthew's chest, hard and
paternal, with his forefinger, over their

lunch of bratwurst and beer. Matthew
spoils the moment, orders tapioca pudding,
takes a mouthful, spits it back

into its cup, takes another mouthful,
spits, mouthful, spits. Later,
in Miami, under Jimmy Johnson, Matthew

dreams of coaching the Dallas Cowboys
someday, authoring a playbook, perhaps
also being the general manager. He asks

Jimmy, "Do G.M.'s select the cheerleaders?"
Jimmy smiles, "It's *the* fucking fringe
benefit." Matthew takes notes, all the time,

an aqua choreography in bright Miami,
wondering if June Taylor is still alive
somewhere along Miami Beach. Would

she teach the Dallas Cowboy Cheerleaders
how to lie on the astro-turf, smile up
to the hole in Texas Stadium's roof,

to the camera's profile, nothing but legs
flaring, phalluses forming the folds
of flowers and vulvas and foam?

Miranda Richardson, or the Cheetah-Woman

Miranda? Miranda, are you awake?

Yes, Matthew.

Do you know the Icelandic word for Cheetah?

Icelandic? Cheetah?

Yeah, what does an Icelander call a cheetah in Icelandic?

*Is Icelandic a language? Don't people in Reykjavic speak some other
language? I mean, don't they call their language something else?*

No, I'm sure it's Icelandic. What else could it be?

*And a cheetah? Why would there be an Icelandic word, a real Icelandic
word, for a cheetah? Where would they run into one?*

We say cheetah, and I was wondering what they say.

But cheetah is hardly an English word, isn't it?

So, you don't know then?

Sorry, love, I have no idea.

> Miranda is falling
> asleep, on their bed, beside
> bowls of figs, black cherries, grapes,
>
> and olives, and it is *Lush
> Life*, Billy Strayhorn, from earlier
> in the evening, that accompanies

Miranda's falling, now through L.A.,
later New York, then London, the usual
homebound arc, through the questions

of "What'll I do next," with
Vivien Haigh-Wood's biography
on the floor. In the morning, she'll

wake quite restful, unblemished,
but now, in this falling, along
her temple and across her thighs

and calves, appear spots, white
then blackening, and then hair,
curling from her vagina, spreading,

over her buttocks, over her legs.
Over her closed eyes, a hint of almonding,
a down-turn in the mouth, but nothing

so definite, and then a slight softening,
fattening of her flesh, slight, across her
belly and torso and breasts, and then

her nipples become blond, flatten,
almost indistinct. As with any
man's, Matthew's penis hardens,

while he watches malefully
with longing. He doesn't touch
the cheetah-woman, this strange

British anthromorph, especially while
she's still falling to her sleep,
after a long day already, after

his silly questions that are a wonder
to her, and a trial, too.
Miranda is in London now,

somewhere between adolescence
and childhood, nowhere near
Iceland or Ireland, and she is

circling in her sleep-dance,
purring in her sleep-fall,
leita, leita, leita.

Why Jerry Kramer Is Not in Barney's *Cremaster 4*

Adapted to maintain the testes at a lower temperature (35°C) than the body temperature (37°C), the scrotum consists of smooth muscle fibers (dartos muscles), which wrinkle the skin of the scrotum, and voluntary muscle fibers (cremaster muscles), which draw the testes upward, closer to the body. The cremaster muscles contract in response to cold temperatures, exercise, or sexual stimulation. In response to warmth, these muscles relax, lowering the testes.

However, there is an anatomical variant in females, where the cremaster muscle is represented by a few fasciculi on the round ligament.

In his research, Matthew Barney
finds a moment in Jerry Kramer's
diary, *Instant Replay*, where

he finds traction, when teen-aged
Kramer, in northern Idaho,
pulls pine splinters lodged in his chest,

perhaps one-inch long. Lombardi,
too, could work, and Lambeau
Field, the hitting the blocking

sled at 10 below, that'll hike
a cremaster to the ceiling. Also
the vision of the quick pulling

guard, between the rolling waves
of run and tackle. But then
the possibilities collapse, Jerry Kramer

doing a stint as a color commentator
for the CFL, and then later,
a spokesman for Intermountain Gas

Company, and his number's all wrong,
64. And what to do with that
singular penetration of that block

thrown on Jethro Pugh, where there's
no circularity, only that one frozen
conclusion? Of course, it has to

be Jim Otto, the O beginning
and the O ending, the bent-over Jim Otto
who'd hike the ball to Daryle Lamonica

or George Blanda, the QB hunched
over those bulbous double zeros,
all boobs, anus, mouth, and vagina.

Otto, the first iron man,
the perennial starter, no matter
the double O scars on each

knee after the replacement surgery,
and still strong enough to man-handle
a young Jack Hamm: The center

who starts the action, again, with
the grip and release of the ball, the second
it goes into another man's hands.

Norman Mailer in the Beehive State

Norman Mailer says, "Houdini?
Good God, I'm an old man!
You want me to play Houdini?"

Matthew points to one storyboard,
a rejected one, where he, Gary Gilmore,
takes the Queen Bee, Salt Lake City

bred and borne. Inside the honeycombed
interior of the great Mormon Tabernacle,
Harry Houdini is straight-jacketed,

and grandson Gary enters and places
the bee on Houdini's great gray forebrow,
and Gary leaves, splitting the vaselined wall's

membrane. Through the wall's wound
fly the drones, after their missions to El Salvador,
Toledo, France, abroad for two years in pairs,

keeping the other straight, and now home,
home, to complete their college years, to have
their BYU fiancèes welcoming them home

with banners of "Welcome Home Elder
Bryan!" and destined to their own planets
in their afterlives, but for now and now

home, home, home, to the Queen Bee
on Norman Mailer's forehead, four thousand
drones, twelve pounds' worth of bees,

landing, pulsing upon his eyelids, the
back of his ears, landing everywhere
there's available flesh. "Wouldn't this

make your cremaster contract?" asks Matthew.
"I'm 75 years old! Don't you know
that? I can hardly get out of this goddamn

chair!" Matthew raises his finger,
"But your cremaster doesn't know the
difference. Your cremaster doesn't

age." And he shows Norman Mailer
the next storyboard. Gary Gilmore,
in prison stripes, wearing a wrestler's

head-gear initialed "B," enters
the honeycombed interior, removes
the queen bee, with the drones flying

off to her again, lifting from the old
Houdini's face, which has not changed,
save for the electricity of wings and

vibrations of lift, and the cremaster
relaxes. For their first time, Norman Mailer's
testicles descend, slowly, finally, down.

Bronco Stadium 1

This is my Bronco Stadium,
before its inaugural game in 1970,
Boise State College vs. Chico State College,

with an ordinary green astro-turf.
Circling the rubber-asphalt track,
a hundred Twyla Tharp human

Pirelli tires, all arms and legs
and radial treads, run, bounce, turn,
all madly wily, an enclosed Route 66.

The tires' spin and run never stop.
The narrative starts with the sky-jumper,
delivering the game ball, floats

to the stadium, as wind vortices sheer
across the field, vacuuming the air
billowing his parachute. He is goalpost

high when the chute collapses,
folds on itself, as a woman's white
skirt, and he falls hard on the turf,

maybe at thirty miles an hour,
destroying his knees, his vertebra,
a stunted stop, and above him

are a thousand more jumpers,
targeting the end zone. In the end zone,
rising from the dressing of the parachute

grows a soft feather of grass, muhly
grass, purpling at its pulp,
and then more sturdy saw grass

grows, taller than the fallen
sky-jumper, who's still waiting
for the Pirelli tires to stop rolling,

for the ambulance to arrive, who can
only raise his arm, cutting his palms
against the serrated edges of grass,

and the grasses spread through
the end zone, down the field's length,
until Bronco Stadium becomes

an islanded Idaho Everglades,
genital-less, a grassy sex of spores
and tendrils, seeds and germination.

The sky jumper on the ground
is paralyzed, and he will stay
that way the rest of his life.

But before the other sky
jumpers land, the wind warms
again, giving them a sure

current to fall into, and as they
fall into the grass, as their chutes
come undone and float away,

they go avian, losing their harnesses
and carabiners and clips,
losing their penises and vulvas,

losing their mammalian
outward sex, their breasts, their nipples,
even losing their hair, their fingers,

until their bodies are only feathered
membranes by which sperm
and egg touch and fall on their own.

Jim Otto Dreams

Otto
oo
Oakland

obituary
Orleans
ottoman

ottoman
ottoman
octopus

Oregon
obsequious
obsidian

offsetting
oxen
opus

opium
oops
Orlando

operational
operatic
open-heart

ovation
ovum
oval

oo
Otto
Otto

orgiastic
Omaha
orgy

offense
orangutan
orgasm

organism
organ
orbital

or
or
Otto

oo
oocyte
obliterate

oracular
ocular
occult

ottomat
ottomatic
ottoman

ottomanic
ottobaun
ottoman

Ontario
old
oo

oo
ornery
osprey

o-man
opal
obelisk

Odessa
odd
odometer

oh
otter
Oslo

omission
Okeechobee
obstinate

oxbow
opulence
orient

oar
o-ring
ocean

oceanic
ocean
ocean

Otto
oo
oo

III. My *Rio Bravo*

It just so happens we be Texicans. Texican is nothin' but a human man way out on a limb, this year and next. Maybe for a hundred more. But I don't think it'll be forever. Some day, this country's gonna be a fine good place to be. Maybe it needs our bones in the ground before that time can come.

Mrs. Jorgensen (Olive Carey), *The Searchers*

Wind Across the Everglades (1958)

I. After the First Dailies—Budd Schulberg Is Pleased by Burl Ives

Burl Ives, yes, God love that fat, pink
s.o.b., God love him for loving
Hemingway and cracker swill, love him
for getting on my ass about Elia Kazan
and HUAC, even when I tell him Jesus
Henry Christ, give it a rest, that's ancient
history, and besides, I tell Burl, I saved
Kazan's soul from that limp-wristed *Streetcar*
romantic hoo-hah, penned *Waterfront*
after Mailer dared me to write a real movie,
which got me the Oscar, a wad of money,
and a way for me and Stuart to do
our own movie, a real Technicolor Florida western,
with sex, strippers, rum, guns, and
bigamists, and I show Burl the real liberal
deal, those gray subplots: 1) the Jewish
shopkeeper and his daughter staking their place
on the frontier, 2) a real Seminole Indian love tragedy,
and 3) the whole conservationist sweep of
the story. Big-hearted Burl, the simp, bear
hugs me. He says he loves me, after I let
him improvise with the rubber moccasin
snake, laughing at what Freud would've made
of it, but happy, he told me, to be playing
the outlaw Cottonmouth, nobody's fool,
and happy that I made the real louses
the Lillie Langtry's and societal belles of London
and New York and their dandified love
of hats and egret feathers and their stupid
husbands, happy, that big-hearted happy soul
God surely has blessed. We trade
shots with the cast, and green Chris
Plummer, who plays the game

warden, is the first to go, until it's just
me and Burl and that sweet fiddling Totch Brown,
who tells us both we'd do fine in
the 'glades. Burl laughs and says, hell, Totch,
we're already here and we're in it for keeps.

II. Budd Schulberg Casts Emmett Kelly

Here's the joke: cast Emmett Kelly, after
Jimmy Stewart stole his role from DeMille,
let him be Bigamy Bob (a sideshow name),
sport a real week's growth beard, besotted
clothes, even a dead felt hat, and the joke,
to give him lines to speak. Kelly talks! And
boy, how he talks, of leaving six wives and
six lawyers behind at the border of the Everglades.
The art of it, too: I write on the script—*no
goddamn ab libbing, no goddamn
jokes!* Kelly plays it straight, as he said he
would when I found him wintering in
Sarasota, as I was trolling among the Ringling
misfits, and there was Emmett Kelly
mixing vodka and orange juice, telling
everyone how this was the right way to enjoy
Florida. He was suspicious at first, unimpressed
with Nick Ray as the director, even with
Gypsy Rose Lee coming out of retirement
to sign on, but he got hooked when I
told him that Tony Galento was going to be in
Burl's gang along with Bigamy Bob. "You know,
Budd," he says, "you're a better boxing writer
than movie writer," and by God, if he isn't
right. Emmett himself saw the genius
in the role, saw how his own life slipped,
not Chaplinesque at all, not even like Keaton,
but a quick slip off the edge of the world.

III. Johnny Guitar

So Ben Gazarra jumps ship as the lead
at the last minute, and here's the classic
Hollywood moment, and I am leaving it
to Nick's gut instinct to cast the right man
as our lawman and who has the romance
of the outlaw in his heart, the right man
big enough to face down Burl Ives, the right
man big enough to be humbled
by the 'glades and learn a thing or two
from the crackers in Chokoloskee. I trust
Nick, and I am thinking *Rebel* and
James Dean, or better, I am thinking *Johnny Guitar*
and Joan Crawford, as hard dressed as any
man, a good and clean shot, a face
you wouldn't cross. Nick says, "Christopher
Plummer." I don't know the guy, and
when he comes off the plane in Miami, I
see the opening scene in the movie, someone
weak and vain, the outsider lawman
coming into town, a little effete, but not too much
Sal Mineo. But in the end, will Plummer do,
someone who's strong enough
for Cottonmouth's poison, strong enough
to break Joan Crawford's neck?

IV. Budd Schulberg at Ted Smallwood's Store

Although Ted's daughter, all southern gritted
and kind, warms to me, or rather, to a man
who doesn't seem all Hollywood and money,
who rightly admires Eisenhower, who hasn't
lost his way, I am looking for the clue here in
this store, where the settlers here killed
Ed Watson, a murderer himself, in 1910. She
says, "I don't remember it at all, but Father,
rest his soul, did not partake in the event."
Years later, Peter Mathiessen asks me
about the movie, my take on Guy Bradley's
death, and tells me he's stitching together
a trilogy of his own on Ed Watson.
Good luck, I tell him. Stuart and I
lost our shirts. Before
production ended, I published the screenplay
for a few extra thousand dollars, to create
a little pre-publicity, to affirm the film,
a strong man's work. It tanked, too. But before
all that muddle, I was standing in Smallwood's store,
smelling the rot of animal carcasses
drying, thinking of the too close
holocaust, and here I stood,
also in the vibrations of another past. Some
men took aim. Everyone fired. A man fell,
dead, before hitting dirt. The star, I knew,
could never be a man, not even Cottonmouth,
but the Everglades, this smell, this color
and its wind.

Baja Florida

—*after Joan Didion*

No Donner Pass this way this century,
no Conestoga wagon-train morality,
        no burying the dead quickly, no tarrying

lest the Indians track you down,
no cautionary tale, no letter from Virginia
        Reed of the Donner Party: *Oh, Mary, I*

    have not wrote you half of the trouble
we've had, but I have wrote you enough
        to let you know what trouble is.

    But thank God, we are the only family
that did not eat human flesh. We have
        left everything, but I don't care for that.

    Don't let this letter dishearten anybody.
Remember, never take no cutoffs
        and hurry along as fast as you can.

But yes, the same abandonments,
this 21st-century crossing, leaving
        Ohio, saying goodbye to all that,

our neighbors who watched the dog,
our job at the bank, the car dealership,
        the high school, our tundra dry snow,

our Church of Our Lady of the Land-
Locked, our inherited season tickets
        at Buckeye Stadium, our ozone filtered

light, our Sycamore and Pin Oak.
Of course, it is not the Ohio
        of our childhood that we abandon,

for these are the things we take with us:
the Thomas Kinkade, Painter of Light ™,
                    prints, the Bible, the plasma

            television set, and the family silver,
and all the rest is down-sized, yard-
                    saled, and tax written-offed, all abandoned

            for that turn-key home. O Cape Coral,
O Bonita Springs, O Estero, O Fort Myers
                    Beach, we have reached this land,

            this Sierra Florida, this Baja Florida,
on the one true road, Interstate 75, to this
                    one true west coast, not taking any shortcuts

            (no passage through Monument Valley,
no saddle-weary Ward Bond, leading
                    the wagon train, bucking up all the greenhorns),

            arriving here as fast as our moving vans
can carry us, and we have reached the end
                    of the line, the end of California.

My *Rio Bravo*

Impossible not to love Dean
        Martin, Dude, then,

                scrounging for the nickel
        for the shot of rot-gut whiskey

the jokester flipped into
        the spittoon that John Wayne

                would kick away, seeing
        what everyone else was seeing:

the celebrity friend, bereft
        of Lewis, not quite making it,

                even with all the favors
        of cameo appearances, record

deals with RCA, and Sinatra
        propping him up, because

                everyone loves Dino, that easy
        wreck anyone of us can careen

into, and when Wayne
        kicks away the spittoon,

                he's kicking it against all
        the weaklings in *High Noon*,

those towns that rely
        on Gary Cooper and all his

                nuances and quiet, towns
        of men who won't back

up their law. Let Grace Kelly
     go to Monte Carlo, or Monaco,

          or any other non-American shore.
     Here on the Rio Bravo, give Wayne

Feathers (sweet,
     edgy Angie Dickinson),

          a woman who gambles
     big, dances bigger, and

later, Howard Hawks will let
     Ricky Nelson sing a duet

          with Dino, just because Hawks
     can make it happen. The killer shot?

The point-of-view from Dude's
     perspective, of John Wayne from

          the boots up, saving us all,
     not giving a damn about why

we're so down and low,
     telling us to get up and get clean.

          We get up, get straight, and no
     longer do we get the shakes,

and then we can kill anyone
     who crosses the sheriff.

Prescribed Burn

I. What is a little fire but destabilization?

Even neutrinos—those mad confederated
waves, hybrid muon, tau, and pure electron,
  oscillating, that shock through everything

material, through light, heat, paper,
through Toby, the bull African elephant
  of the Cincinnati Zoo, through Virginia

Woolf's ashes, through the sun's
own core—the neutrinos themselves
  would amount to nothing if it weren't

for those aberrant manifestations that
momentarily hold mass and then let
  it go, those reckless, impulsive

lottery winners who buy the store and
give away all the Barbie dolls to thieves
  and musicians just because they

can, once more nearly penniless, happy,
going back to the 7-11 and buying a new
  ticket. Of the safe, respectable, constant

neutrinos, no fire then, for sure, no star stew,
no combustion, just a cool, interminable
  equilibrium, silence, a sure baseline.

II. Where have you secreted your pyromania?

Funny, it's *play* with matches, so that
in your backyard, piling leaves
          and sticks, near your father's picket

fence, fire becomes a game of light
and color, an improvised smokiness,
          a music of tinder cracking. Forget

Prometheus. Forget witchcraft.
Forget the physics of accelerated decay
          and released energy. It's a matter

of blowing into the roots of fire,
letting the fire recover, burn hotter,
          and then blowing again, until the fire

itself takes over, and you can rest
from the dizziness, watch the flames
          lick the panels of wood, and climb.

III. *Do you know your escape route from your bedroom?*

Pick up your cell phone, call Carl Hutchinson,
the representative from the Grabic Finance
       Agency, who manages your retirement annuity

     and 401k plans. Carl says, "Sure, I'll be
there immediately," and he arrives pronto,
       beneath your second-floor bedroom window,

     following your directions to a tee. He piles
bundles of twenty-dollar bills on the ground,
       all $47,000 worth liquidated from your account,

     minus penalties for early withdrawal and
taxes withheld, forming a tidy mound, no larger
       than the carapace of a full-grown gopher tortoise,

     and Carl takes in one breath, steps and ascends
the pile of your dough, shouts above the flames,
       "I can't reach you! I can't reach you! What now?"

IV. Why should you prevent forest fires?

The speed of fire is a simple equation,
a curve a good 11th-grade student
   could express. But more exact is

  the equation to cheat an insurance
company, to win back an investment
   with a little vengeance. Think of

  Mickey Rourke warning William Hurt
against arson in *Body Heat*, and
   of course, Hurt burns everything

  and murders Richard Crenna. Or
rather, think of the film itself
   of *Body Heat*, burning itself up,

  cracking and fading, three hundred years
from now, or think of the DVD itself
   of *Body Heat*, unloosening its digital

  coding, the binary relations ashened,
one thousand years from now. It is
   the vanity of self-immolation that

  I can't stand, the shower of the accelerant
over the body, the striking of the match,
   and then the poof of holiness:

  the concentration and silence against
the flesh as it drips in tiny globes
   of flame. That way is one answer,

  to burn away the self, cleansing
the corruption, to do something. Too
   much burning for God, for money,

for love, unless you are the Elvis,
American-sainted, draped in your Phoenix
                cape, red-sequined and diamond-studded,

                and you turn your back to your audience,
raise your arms, and behind you, you
                can hear women faint from the heat.

Notes

Matthew Barney is the current "It" artist—he has become important enough so that it is now fashionable to criticize his work. Barney was born in San Francisco and moved with his family to Boise, my hometown, when he was six. He played football and wrestled in high school, and he led Capital High School to the 1985 State Championship as the star quarterback. His seminal work is the five-part film series *Cremaster Cycle* (1994-2002).

"Bronco Stadium 3": Barney sequences his work in non-numeric order. This poem narrates, with minimal embellishment, Barney's *Cremaster I*.

"If Matthew Barney Were 6'3"" and "Miranda Richardson, or the Cheetah-Woman": These two poems invent a parallel life for Barney, imagining if he were three inches taller and had a shot at a professional football career. The romance with Miranda Richardson is a complete fiction, but it's nice to think about. In the early 1990s, she won attention for a number of films, especially her work in *The Crying Game*, as an IRA terrorist (Ireland does figure into Barney's *Cremaster Cycle*), which led to her role of Viv Eliot in *Tom and Viv*. *Leita* is not Icelandic for cheetah, but for another word, *word*.

"Norman Mailer in the Beehive State": Like many non-Mormon Idahoans, especially those raised in the southern part of the state, Barney has an ambivalent fascination with Mormonism, which he explores in his work. He also has fascinations with Masonic imagery, the Isle of Man, prosthetics, Vaseline, tap dancing goat man, bulls and salt, dancing women in lamb outfits, the Chrysler building, internment, Budapest, etc.

"Bronco Stadium 1": I attended the first football game played at the current Bronco Stadium in 1970 (I also played in Bronco Stadium that year as a defensive end for my Optimist Little League football team, Mountain Bell, in the league's championship game). The depiction of the parachutist falling to the turf as he delivered the inaugural game ball, resulting in his paralysis, is accurate, except he landed near mid-field rather than in the end zone.

"Jim Otto Dreams": Jim Otto, the center for the Oakland Raiders, is an important emblem in Barney's early work, for his constancy, his work ethic, and his impossibly amazing fortitude.

"Winds Across the Everglades (1958)"

Why you can get *Madam Satan* (1930) on VHS and DVD and not *Winds Across the Everglades* is beyond me. Budd Schulberg, with his brother Stuart as co-producer and Nicholas Ray as the director, pieced together a remarkable and improbable movie about a conservation warden, a Jewish shop-keeper and his daughter, two Seminole lovers, and a band of renegade plume hunters, filmed on location at Everglades City. The movie is in glorious Technicolor, and features all the actors mentioned in the sequence—not mentioned, and I don't know why I didn't include him, because I love him in the way everyone else does, is Peter Falk, as the Writer. I haven't seen the movie either, but I read the screenplay, which Schulberg published to promote the movie.

"Baja Florida"

This poem was triggered by my reading Joan Didion's *Where I Was From*.

About the Author

James Brock is the author of two previous books of poetry, *The Sunshine Mine Disaster* (University of Idaho Press) and *nearly Florida* (Anhinga Press). For his poetry, he has won fellowships from the National Endowment for the Arts, the Alex Haley Foundation, the Tennessee Arts Commission, and the Idaho Commission for the Arts. He currently is a professor of English at Florida Gulf Coast University in Fort Myers, Florida, where he enjoys birding and film. After he dies, his spirit will go with Hope Lange to Manhattan in 1957, drink cocktails and trade smokes with Joan Crawford, wear Edith Head suits and pajamas, all in his *The Best of Everything* afterlife.

Printed in the United States
119775LV00003B/310-327/A